The Power of Your Tongue

7Days

Daily Declarations of Faith, Strength, and Provision over your Life!

Pastor Michael Brown

Copyright © 2023 Pastor Michael Brown

All rights reserved.

It is strictly forbidden to replicate, copy, or otherwise distribute any of the material presented in this book without first obtaining explicit and written permission from either the author or the publisher.

Eagles Gathering International

Ministry London Uk

Tel: +44 20 8126 1431

Website:

www.egiministry.com

www.egiministry.org

SPECIAL THANKS TO

My Wife Pastor Angela Brown. She helped me a lot to publish this book.

Table Of Contents

Introduction 7

Day One Sunday: Faith 11

Day Two Monday: Strength 15

Day Three Tuesday: Peace 19

Day Four Wednesday: Joy 23

Day Five Thursday: Love 27

Day Six Friday: Wisdom 31

Day Seven Saturday: Provision 35

Conclusion 39

INTRODUCTION

Declarations: Speaking God's Truth Over Your Life" suggests that the book is a manual for speaking God's promises and truth over one's life on a daily basis. The goal of daily declarations is to strengthen one's foundation of faith and rejuvenate one's thinking with God's Word. One can align their thoughts and behaviors with God's will by proclaiming the truth of His Word, and they will then experience the blessings and provision He has promised. Because words have power and when we speak the truth of God's Word over our life, it can result in good change and transformation, daily declarations are crucial.

Daily affirmations can aid in the development of a regular routine for speaking life, truth, and encouragement over our lives. Declaring the truth of God's Word causes us to align ourselves with His will and invite His power into our lives because words have the ability to influence our thoughts, emotions, and behavior.

Through daily declarations, we can also overcome negative thought patterns and limiting beliefs that hold us back from living the abundant life God has for us. By replacing negative self-talk with declarations of faith, strength, peace, and provision, we can experience transformation in our minds and hearts.

The fact that daily declarations foster a closer relationship with God is another significant benefit of doing them. We meditate on His Word as we proclaim His truth over our life, welcoming His presence and direction into our every day. As we come to accept God's plan for our lives, this can bring about a greater sense of serenity, joy, and purpose.

In summary, daily declarations are an important tool for renewing our minds, aligning ourselves with God's will, and cultivating a deeper relationship with Him. By speaking His truth over our lives each day, we can experience transformation, freedom, and abundant life in Christ.

Dear reader,

I want to exhort you to profess your belief in God's promises and His power to fulfill them. The Bible states that "God is not a man, that He should lie, nor a son of man, that He should repent. Has He said, and will He not do? Or has He spoken, and will He not make it good?" (Numbers 23:19). God has the ability to fulfill His promises in our lives, so we can have confidence that they are genuine.

I am aware that, on sometimes, it might be challenging to put our faith in God's promises, particularly when we are dealing with trying situations or persistent difficulties. But even when it seems like nothing is changing, I want to encourage you to cling to your faith and speak God's promises over your life.

Declare that God keeps His word and that He will bring His plans to pass in His own time. Declare your belief that God will use everything for your good and that you trust His plan for your life (Romans 8:28).

When you declare faith in God's promises, you are aligning yourself with His will and inviting His power into your life. Additionally, you are boosting your own faith and laying a solid foundation of faith in God that will see you through every adversity and difficulty.

Therefore, I urge you to express your faith in God's promises and His capacity to fulfill them today. Declare your faith in God's unwavering love, His wisdom, and His ability to work in and through your life. And be aware that by doing so, you are allowing God to shower you with all the benefits and provisions He has in store for you.

May God bless you abundantly as you declare your faith in Him and His promises.

Sincerely,

Pastor Michael Brown

DAY ONE SUNDAY:

FAITH

Declare your belief in God's promises and in His capacity to fulfill them.

Declaring our confidence in God's promises and His capacity to fulfill them is a potent act that has the power to change our lives. Speaking God's promises aloud brings us into alignment with His will and opens the door for His power to work in our lives. Additionally, we are fortifying our own faith and laying a solid foundation of faith in God, which will see us through every trial and difficulty. When we are dealing with challenging circumstances, it might be challenging to trust in God's promises, but by expressing our faith in Him and His promises, we are reminding ourselves of His unwavering love, His discernment, and His ability to work in our lives. We make ourselves available to accept all the gifts and provisions that God has in store for us as we continue to express confidence in His promises.

CONFESSIONS SCRIPTURES

Hebrews 11:1 - "Now faith is the substance of things hoped for, the evidence of things not seen."

Mark 11:24 - "Therefore I say unto you, what things soever ye desire when ye pray, believe that ye receive them, and ye shall have them."

Romans 4:20-21 - "He staggered not at the promise of God through unbelief; but was strong in faith, giving glory to God; And being fully persuaded that, what he had promised, he was able also to perform."

DECLARATION PRAYER POINTS

Ask God to increase your faith and help you trust Him more

1. Oh Lord, good morning.
2. Lord Jesus, I am grateful for the gift of life and the chance to begin a fresh day. In Jesus Name
3. Oh Lord, I declare that I am blessed today and that I will encounter Your goodness in all facets of my life. In Jesus' Name.
4. Oh Lord, I know you are my parent and have wonderful intentions for me In Jesus' Name.
5. Lord Jesus, I decided to rely on your word and keep your promises as a result. In Jesus Name
6. Oh Lord according to Psalm 37:4, Put your trust in the Lord, and He will grant you your heart's desires. In Jesus' Name.
7. Oh Lord, from this day In the Mighty Name of Jesus, I make the decision to take pleasure in you today and put my faith in your ability to provide my heart's wishes by your will. In Jesus' Name.
8. Oh Lord, I know you have excellent things in store for me, and I gratefully accept them. In Jesus' Name.
9. By the blood of Jesus, I also announce that you have defended me from all of the enemy's malicious schemes. For He shall give His angels charge over thee, to keep thee in all thy ways, according to Psalm 91:11 in thy word. In Jesus' Name.

10. Oh God, I put my faith in your protection and am confident that no plan you devise will succeed against me. In Jesus' Name.
11. Lord Jesus, as I begin this day, Father, I pray for wisdom and direction. In Jesus' Name.
12. Oh Lord as your word said, If anyone among you lacks wisdom, let him ask of God, who gives to everyone generously and without reproach, and it will be given to him, In Jesus' Name.
13. Oh Lord, according to James 1:5. I beseech you for the wisdom to walk in your ways and make the proper decisions. In Jesus' Name.
14. Mighty God of battle, I give you this day, and I beg you to go before me and straighten every crooked route. "In Jesus' Name.
15. Mighty God, your word says in (Proverbs 3:6) "'In all your ways acknowledge Him, and He shall guide your paths," In Jesus' Mighty Name.
16. Lord Jesus, as I make the decision to thank you for all I do today, I have faith that you will guide me. In Jesus' Name, I pray Amen.

DAY TWO MONDAY:

STRENGTH

Declare that you have strength through Christ and can do all things through Him.

When we declare that we have strength through Christ and can do all things through Him, we are acknowledging the power and ability that comes from our relationship with Him. According to Philippians 4:13, "I can do all things through Christ which strengthened me." This proclamation serves as a reminder that we have access to the strength and power of the living God and that we are not alone in our troubles. We can have confidence that Christ is with us and will enable us to overcome and overcome any obstacles we may encounter. Declaring our strength in Him gives us access to a force greater than our own, giving us assurance that we won't be overcome by our circumstances. May we constantly exalt Christ as our strength and put our faith in His capacity to guide us through every circumstance we encounter.

CONFESSIONS SCRIPTURES

According to Philippians 4:13 - "I can do all things through Christ which strengtheneth me."

Isaiah 40:31 states - "But they that wait upon the Lord shall renew their strength; they shall mount up with wings as eagles; they shall run, and not be weary; and they shall walk, and not faint."

2 Timothy 1:7 - "For God hath not given us the spirit of fear; but of power, and of love, and of a sound mind."

DECLARATION PRAYER POINTS

To the extent possible, rely on God's strength and guidance rather than your own.

1. Thank you, Lord, for another day of life. You have made this day, In Jesus' Name.
2. Oh Lord by the Blood of Jesus, I declare, and I will rejoice and be glad, In Jesus' Name.
3. Oh Loed, According to Philippians 4:4, your word, "Rejoice in the Lord always: and again, I say, Rejoice." I choose to rejoice in you today and every day. In Jesus' Mighty Name
4. 4 Blood of Jesus. I declare by the power of God, that the scars of Jesus Christ have made me whole.in Jesus' Name.
5. Oh Lord According to Isaiah 53:5, states "But he was wounded for our transgressions, he was bruised for our iniquities: the chastisement of our peace was upon him; and with his stripes, we are healed."In Jesus' Name.
6. Oh Lord, By Your Blood, you have the power to heal my body, mind, and spirit so that I am free from illness and disease. In Jesus' Name.
7. Mighty God, I beg you to grant me the courage to face every obstacle in my path. In Jesus Name
8. Oh Lord, according to Philippians 4:13 of your word, "I can do all things through Christ who strengthens me." In Jesus' Mighty Name.
9. Holy Ghost Fire, I proclaim in the name of Jesus that I am an overcomer. In Jesus' Name.

10. Lord Jesus, I confirm that I am fortunate enough to be a blessing. In Jesus Name
11. Oh Lord, I Speak Genesis 12:2 over my life "And I will make of thee a great nation, and I will bless thee, and make thy name great, and thou shalt be a blessing." In Jesus Name
12. Lord Jesus, I decided to spread your blessings through me to people around me, and I have faith that you will use me to change lives and better the world. In Jesus' Name.
13. Lord Jesus, I give you this day and beg that you direct my ways and lead me down the correct path. In Jesus Name
14. Oh Lord, according to Psalm 23:3 " You restoreth my soul: You leadeth me in the paths of righteousness for your name's sake."
15. Oh Lord, I've decided to go with your direction and have faith that you'll take me to my Place of blessing, In Jesus' Name.

Day Three Tuesday:

Peace

Declare that you have peace that surpasses all understanding because you trust in God.

When We acknowledge the influence of God's presence in our life when we say that we have peace that passes all comprehension as a result of our trust in Him. According to Philippians 4:7,"And the peace of God, which passeth all understanding, shall keep your hearts and minds through Christ Jesus." This affirmation serves as a reminder that God is worthy of our confidence and is devoted to giving us an indescribable serenity. We may trust that God will be with us through all of our difficulties, leading and upholding us. Declaring our faith in Him enables us to feel a profound serenity that dispels our worries, soothes our fears, and fortifies our souls. In the mighty name of Jesus, may we continually exclaim our faith in God and find tranquility that is beyond all comprehension.

CONFESSIONS SCRIPTURES

Philippians 4:7 - "And the peace of God, which passeth all understanding, shall keep your hearts and minds through Christ Jesus."

John 14:27 - "Peace I leave with you, my peace I give unto you: not as the world giveth, give I unto you. Let not your heart be troubled, neither let it be afraid."

Isaiah 26:3 - "Thou wilt keep him in perfect peace, whose mind is stayed on thee: because he trusteth in thee."

DECLARATION PRAYER POINTS

Pray to God to give you His peace and to assist you in letting go of stress and tension.

1. Lord Jesus, I give thanks to you, Father, for the unfathomable tranquility. In Jesus Name
2. Lord Jesus, according to Philippians 4:7, "And the peace of God, which surpasses all understanding, will guard your hearts and minds through Christ Jesus."
3. Lord Jesus, Even in the midst of instability and disorder, I decided to put my faith in your serenity. In Jesus' Name.
4. Oh Lord I announce that you have given me peace and that I have faith that you are in charge of everything. In Jesus' Name.
5. Oh Lord, I confess that the blood of Jesus Christ has covered my sins and purchased my redemption. In Jesus' Name.
6. Oh Lord, According to Colossians 1:14, your word. "In whom we have redemption through his blood, even the forgiveness of sins."
7. Lord Jesus, I accept your forgiveness and grace, and I make the decision to live out the freedom you have granted me. In Jesus' Name.
8. Father, I pray that you will favor my encounters and my relationships with others today. In Jesus' Mighty Name.
9. Oh Lord, I Speak Proverbs 16:7 over my life, "When a man's ways please the Lord, he maketh even his enemies to be at peace with him."
10. Oh Lord I decide to respect you in my interactions and I have faith that you will promote harmony In Jesus' Name...

11. Oh Lord, I announce that I am wealthy and blessed monetarily. In Jesus' Name.
12. Lord Jesus, Deuteronomy 8:18 in your word states, "And thou shalt remember the Lord thy God: for it is he that giveth thee power to get wealth, that he may establish his covenant which he sware unto thy fathers, as it is this day." In Jesus Name
13. Almighty God, I accept your wealth and provision, and I have faith that you will favor the creations of my hands. In Jesus' Name.
14. Almighty God, I devote this day to you, Father, and I beg you to anoint me with your Holy Spirit and give me the strength to serve as a testimony for you. In Jesus' Name.
15. Oh Lord, I confirm Acts 1:8. "But ye shall receive power, after that the Holy Ghost has come upon you: and ye shall be witnesses unto me both in Jerusalem, and in all Judaea, and in Samaria, and unto the uttermost part of the earth." In Jesus' Name.
16. Oh Lord, I make the decision to serve as a conduit for your kingdom and to show others your love and the truth. In Jesus' Name, Amen

Day Four Wednesday:

Joy

When We express our gladness in the Lord even in trying situations by asserting our faith in His goodness and constancy. According to Psalm 16:11 "Thou wilt shew me the path of life: in thy presence is fulness of joy; at thy right hand there are pleasures for evermore." This statement serves as a reminder that our ability to be joyful is not based on external circumstances, but rather on our connection with God. No matter what difficulties we may encounter, we may be sure that God will be there to help, direct, and provide for us. We are drawing from a source of joy that is larger than our own when we express our joy in Him, and we can be sure that we won't let our circumstances win. May we never cease to rejoice in the Lord and put our faith in His capacity to guide us through whatever circumstance we encounter.

CONFESSIONS SCRIPTURES

Nehemiah 8:10 - "Then he said unto them, Go your way, eat the fat, and drink the sweet, and send portions unto them for whom nothing is prepared: for this day is holy unto our Lord: neither be ye sorry; for the joy of the Lord is your strength."

Psalm 16:11 - "Thou wilt shew me the path of life: in thy presence is fulness of joy; at thy right hand there are pleasures for evermore."

James 1:2-4 - "My brethren, count it all joy when ye fall into divers temptations; Knowing this, that the trying of your faith worketh patience. But let patience have her perfect work, that ye may be perfect and entire, wanting nothing."

DECLARATION PRAYER POINTS

Ask God to fill you with His joy and help you find joy in Him, not just in earthly things

1. Lord, I praise you for your steadfast love and fidelity. In the Name of Jesus.
2. Lamentations 3:22–23, according to your word, "It is of the Lord's mercies that we are not consumed because his compassions fail not. They are new every morning: great is thy faithfulness." In the Name of Jesus. '' Hallelujah''
3. Lord Jesus, I decided to put my faith in your constancy, and I am sure that you won't ever abandon me. In the Name of Jesus.
4. Oh Lord, I acknowledge that I am a child of God and that I have confidence in your love, In the Name of Jesus.
5. Lord Jesus. as stated in 1 John 3:1, "Behold, what manner of love the Father hath bestowed upon us, that we should be called the sons of God." In the Name of Jesus.
6. Oh Lord, I accept your love and make the decision to live up to the identity you have given me. In the Name of Jesus.
7. Holy Ghost Fire, shields my mind from all dread and unfavorable thoughts. In the Name of Jesus.
8. Lord Jesus, in 2 Timothy 1:17, according to your word, "For God hath not given us the spirit of fear; but of power, and of love, and of a sound mind." In the Name of Jesus.

9. Oh Lord, I decide to keep my attention on your truth and have faith in the ability to face every fear by the power of God. In the Name of Jesus.
10. Mighty God, I declare to you, Father, that I am joyful and at rest. In the Name of Jesus.
11. Oh Lord, Romans 15:13, according to your word "Now the God of hope fill you with all joy and peace in believing, that ye may abound in hope, through the power of the Holy Ghost." In the Name of Jesus.
12. Lord Jesus, I accept your happiness and peace, and I decide to live out the hope you have given me. In the Name of Jesus.
13. Father God, I give you all the glory in your mighty name, Lord, and I surrender this day to you. In Jesus' Name.

Day Five Thursday:

Love

When One of the cornerstones of the Christian faith is affirmed when we affirm that we are loved by God and that His love flows through us to others. John 3:16, an example "For God so loved the world, that he gave his only begotten Son, that whosoever believeth in him should not perish, but have everlasting life." When we say that God loves us, we are stating that His love for us is not based on how good we are or how deserving we are, but rather on His character and His grace. This affirmation also serves as a reminder that, as 1 John 4:7-8 states, we are obligated to spread His love to others. "Beloved, let us love one another: for love is of God; and everyone that loveth is born of God, and knoweth God. He that loveth not knoweth not God; for God is love." May we never stop proclaiming God's love for us and working to spread that love to others, realizing that it is only because of His love that we can show love to and serve others around us.

CONFESSIONS SCRIPTURES

1 John 4:19 - "We love him because he first loved us."

John 13:34-35 - "A new commandment I give unto you, That ye love one another; as I have loved you, that ye also love one another. By this shall all men know that ye are my disciples if ye have love one to another."

1 Corinthians 13:4-7 - "Charity suffereth long, and is kind; charity envieth not; charity vaunteth not itself, is not puffed up, Doth not

behave itself unseemly, seeketh not her own, is not easily provoked, thinketh no evil; Rejoiceth not in iniquity, but rejoiceth in the truth; Beareth all things, believeth all things, hopeth all things, endureth all things."

DECLARATION PRAYER POINTS

Ask God to make His love a part of you so that you might love others, even those who are challenging to love.

1. Lord Jesus, I sincerely appreciate your mercy and grace, Father. Hebrews 4:16 states in Your word. "Let us, therefore, come boldly unto the throne of grace, that we may obtain mercy, and find grace to help in time of need." In the Mighty Name of Jesus.
2. Lord Jesus, I confidently approach you today, pleading for your forgiveness and grace to see me through every difficulty. In the Name of Jesus.
3. Oh Lord, I declare that through Christ Jesus, I have overcome every stubborn situation in my life. In the Name of Jesus.
4. Oh Lord, According to 1 John 5:4 in your word "For whatsoever is born of God overcometh the world: and this is the victory that overcometh the world, even our faith." In the Name of Jesus.
5. In the Name of Jesus, I decided to move on in faith and to have faith that you have given me the ability to overcome every challenge in my life. In the Name of Jesus.
6. Father God, I beg you to direct my steps and set my course. In the Name of Jesus.
7. Father God, according to your word in Proverbs 3:5–6, I must "Trust in the Lord with all thine heart; and lean not unto thine

own understanding. In all thy ways acknowledge him, and he shall direct thy paths." In the Name of Jesus.
8. Father God, I decided to put my faith in you and follow your directions because I know that you will lead me in the part of righteousness. In the Name of Jesus.
9. Holy Fire, I announce, that Jesus Christ's stripes have cured me from every (pick from the list bellow) and command them to break now, by the blood of Jesus

Every satanic cancer

Every satanic pneumonia:

Every diabetes:

Every satanic allergy:

Every satanic migraine:

Every satanic depression:

Every satanic Influenza:

Every satanic anxiety:

Every satanic fever

Every satanic ulcer:

Every satanic arthritis:

Every satanic heart disease:

10. Oh Lord, I speak 1 Peter 2:24, over my life, according to your word, "Who his own self bare our sins in his own body on the tree, that we, being dead to sins, should live unto righteousness: by whose stripes ye were healed." In the Name of Jesus.

11. Father God, I vow that I am whole in you as I accept your healing power. In the Name of Jesus.
12. Father God, I give this day up to you, Father, and ask that you use me in a way that brings you honor. In the Name of Jesus.
13. Lord Jesus, according to your word in Matthew 5:16, "Let your light so shine before men, that they may see your good works, and glorify your Father which is in heaven." In the Name of Jesus.
14. Oh Lord, I decided to shine in you, and I have faith that you will use me to improve the lives of others in my immediate vicinity. In Jesus' name, I pray. Amen

Day Six Friday:

Wisdom

Declare that you have wisdom from God and that you seek His guidance in all things.

Proverbs 2:6 states that "the Lord giveth wisdom: out of his mouth cometh knowledge and understanding." We acknowledge that true wisdom originates with God and not from our own understanding when we claim to have insight from Him and ask for His direction in everything. We can only make wise decisions and face life's obstacles by asking for His direction and depending on His wisdom. James 1:5 tells this, "If any of you lack wisdom, let him ask of God, that giveth to all men liberally, and upbraideth not; and it shall be given him." Declaring our reliance on God for insight allows us to be open to receiving the wisdom and direction that only He can give. Let's declare this every day, putting our faith in His wisdom to lead us through every situation and choice we have to make.

CONFESSIONS SCRIPTURES

James 1:5 - "If any of you lack wisdom, let him ask of God, that giveth to all men liberally, and upbraideth not; and it shall be given him."

Proverbs 3:5-6 - "Trust in the Lord with all thine heart; and lean not unto thine own understanding. In all thy ways acknowledge him, and he shall direct thy paths."

1 Corinthians 1:30 - "But of him are ye in Christ Jesus, who of God is made unto us wisdom, and righteousness, and sanctification, and redemption."

DECLARATION PRAYER POINTS

Ask God to grant you wisdom and to guide you in all of your life's decisions.

1. Oh Lord, I give you thanks for your counsel and insight. by the Blood of Jesus.
2. Oh Lord according to James 1:5, your word. "If any of you lack wisdom, let him ask of God, that giveth to all men liberally, and upbraideth not; and it shall be given him." In the Name of Jesus.
3. Oh Lord I come to you today, trusting that you would guide me in the correct direction, asking for your wisdom and insight. In the Name of Jesus.
4. Mighty God, I declare that I am a tool for your kingdom and that your Holy Spirit gives me strength. In Jesus' Name.
5. Today Lord Jesus, I declared over my life, Acts 2:38 of your word states that "Then Peter said unto them, Repent, and be baptized every one of you in the name of Jesus Christ for the remission of sins, and ye shall receive the gift of the Holy Ghost." In Jesus' Name.
6. Today Lord Jesus, I accept your Holy Spirit and decide to serve as a conduit for your heavenly kingdom. In the Name of Jesus Christ.
7. Oh Lord, please keep me and my loved ones safe from all plans of the enemies. In the Name of Jesus.
8. Holy Ghost Fire, Lord, according to Psalm 91:11–12 in your word, "For he shall give his angels charge over thee, to keep

thee in all thy ways. They shall bear thee up in their hands, lest thou dash thy foot against a stone." in Jesus Mighty Name.

9. Oh Lord. I put my faith in your vigilance and find solace in the security of your affection. In the Name of Jesus.
10. Lord Jesus, I announce that you have blessed me and are pleased with me, In the Name of Jesus.
11. Lord Jesus, I prophesy. Psalm 5:12 over my life, "For thou, Lord, wilt bless the righteous; with favor wilt thou compass him as with a shield." In the Name of Jesus.
12. Lord Jesus, I accept your favor and blessing, and I put my faith in you to open up for me doors by the Blood of Jesus that no one will be able to close. In the Name of Jesus.
13. Holy Ghost, I give this day to the Lord, and I ask you to use me for your glory. In the Mighty Name of Jesus

DAY SEVEN SATURDAY:

PROVISION

Declare that you trust God to supply all of your needs and that He is your provider.

As believers, We can confidently affirm that God is our provider and that we put our complete trust in Him to supply all of our needs. The apostle Paul reminds us in Philippians 4:19 that "my God shall supply all your need according to his riches in glory by Christ Jesus." By affirming that God is our provider, we acknowledge that He is the source of all good things and that we rely on Him to supply all of our needs, whether they be material, psychological, or spiritual. Even in trying or uncertain circumstances, we can put our faith in His constancy to provide for us. We can have peace knowing that God is our loving Father who looks out for us and will always meet our needs by repeating this affirmation daily.

CONFESSIONS SCRIPTURES

Philippians 4:19 - "But my God shall supply all your need according to his riches in glory by Christ Jesus."

Matthew 6:33 - "But seek ye first the kingdom of God, and his righteousness; and all these things shall be added unto you."

Psalm 23:1 - "The Lord is my shepherd; I shall not want."

DECLARATION PRAYER POINTS

Ask God to provide for all your needs and help you trust Him to do so

1. Lord, I praise you for your fullness and provision. In Jesus Name
2. Heavenly Father, according to Philippians 4:19 in your word, "But my God shall supply all your need according to his riches in glory by Christ Jesus." In Jesus' Mighty Name.
3. My God of Miracles, I have faith in your ability to provide all of my wants, and I am appreciative of your abundance in my life. In the Name of Jesus.
4. My God of Miracles, I hereby announce that through Christ Jesus, I am victorious. In the Name of Jesus.
5. You God of All my Battles, I speak the word of Romans 8:37 over my life today, "Nay, in all these things I (PUT YOUR NAME I THE BLANK SPACE)………………….…..are more than conquerors through him that loved us." In the Name of Jesus Christ.
6. Lord Jesus, I decided to walk in triumph, sure that I can get over any challenge put in my path. In the Name of Jesus.
7. Lord Jesus, please grant me the confidence to follow my purpose and to step out by faith, In the Name of Jesus
8. Joshua 1:9 in your word states, "Have not I commanded thee? Be strong and of good courage; be not afraid, neither be thou dismayed: for the Lord thy God is with thee whithersoever thou goest." In the Name of Jesus
9. Lord Jesus, I decided to put my faith in you and to walk with the confidence that comes from knowing you are by my side. In the Name of Jesus.

10. Oh Lord, I announce that your Holy Spirit has anointed me by the power of the Holy Ghost. In the Name of Jesus
11. Lord Jesus, In your word, 1 John 2:27, "But the anointing which ye have received of him abideth in you, and ye need not that any man teaches you: but as the same anointing teacheth you of all things, and is truth, and is no lie, and even as it hath taught you, ye shall abide in him." In the Name of Jesus
12. Oh Lord, I accept your anointing and decide to follow your Spirit's guidance. In the Name of Jesus
13. Lord Jesus, I give this day to you, and I beg you to use me for your glory. According to Ephesians 2:10 in your word, "For we are his workmanship, created in Christ Jesus unto good works, which God hath before ordained that we should walk in them." In Jesus' Mighty Name

Conclusion

In conclusion, declaring the Word of God over our lives is a powerful tool for strengthening our faith and renewing our minds. Speaking the Bible aloud affirms its truth and invites God's power and presence into our lives. The Bible is alive and active. We can develop a closer relationship with God, replenish our brains with His truth, and live in His bountiful benefits by making daily professions of faith.

Dear reader, I implore you to keep speaking the Word of God over your life. As you proclaim His truth and promises over every aspect of your life, may you be overflowing with faith, hope, and love. And may you be a light to those around you, encouraging them to declare the Word of God over their lives as well. May you experience His peace, joy, and power in the midst of every hardship. Keep in mind that by declaring His truth and promises, you are committing to His will and purpose for your life, and He is faithful to carry it out. Continue speaking out His Word as He changes your life from the inside out.

It's critical to keep in mind that the authority of God's Word is what gives our assertions their force. As we speak the Scriptures over our lives, we are asking God's presence and power to act in and through us. The Scriptures are an effective tool for transformation. God's promises are true and trustworthy, and by reciting His Word, we are putting ourselves in line with His will and purpose for our lives. Therefore, let us keep speaking His truth and promises over our lives, knowing that by doing so we are strengthening our faith, refreshing our thoughts, and experiencing His countless blessings. As you continue to announce God's truth and promises over your life, may the truth of His Word serve as a light for you to follow and a source of strength.

Finally, as we draw to a close, I want to exhort you to pray, read the Bible, and go to church in order to develop a closer connection with God. I pray that this journey of daily declarations has encouraged and equipped you to put your faith in God's promises, speak His truth over your life, and experience the fullness of His power and love. Keep in mind that the truth of God's Word is the source of the power of your declarations, and as you line your words with His truth, you will experience His kindness and faithfulness in your life. So, continue proclaiming His truth, pursuing Him with all of your heart, and placing your faith in His unfailing love and provision for your needs. As you proceed on this spiritual path, may God richly bless you, and may the grace and peace of our Lord Jesus Christ surround you at all times.

Made in the USA
Columbia, SC
19 October 2023